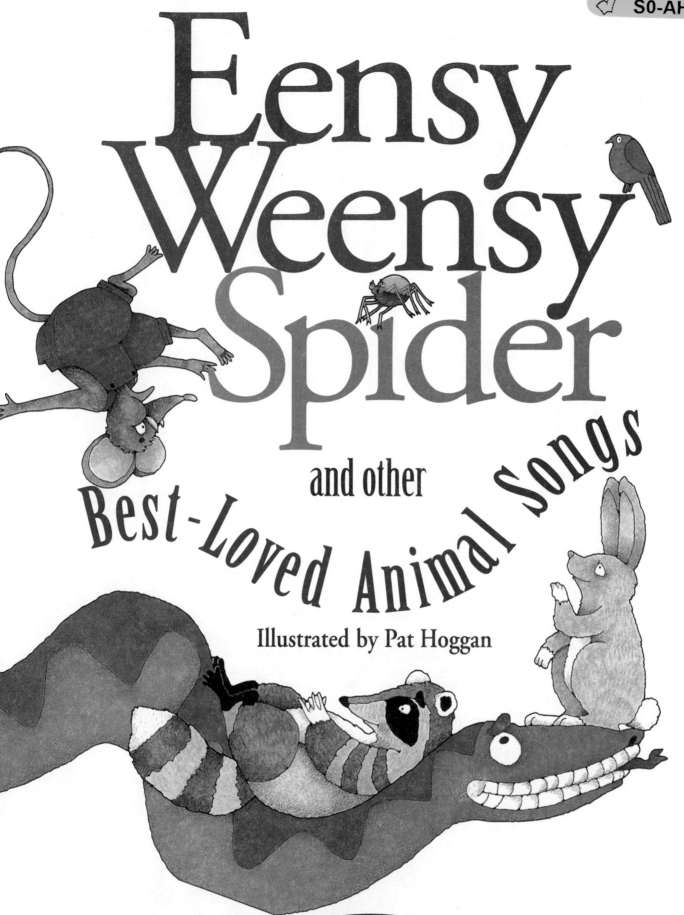

Eensy Weensy Spider

and other

Best-Loved Animal Songs

Illustrated by Pat Hoggan

Troll

This edition published in 2000.

Words and music for "Animals" and "Animal March" by George James.

Original arrangements for all other titles by George James.

The publisher wishes to thank Randa Kirshbaum for her transcriptions of these original music arrangements.

Text copyright © 1993 by Troll Communications L.L.C.

Illustration copyright © 1993 by Pat Hoggan.

ISBN 0-8167-6983-4

Printed in the United States of America.

10 9 8 7 6 5 4 3 2

Contents

Animals

Relaxed

Words and music by George James

Chorus

An - i - mals, an - i - mals, let's all talk a - bout an - i - mals.

An - i - mals, an - i - mals, let's all sing a - bout an - i - mals. Some

growl, some bark,— some go walk - ing in a park.— There are

those who wait 'til dark to say, "Who? Yes, you." Some

laugh, some sing. Some don't sound like an - y - thing. Some make

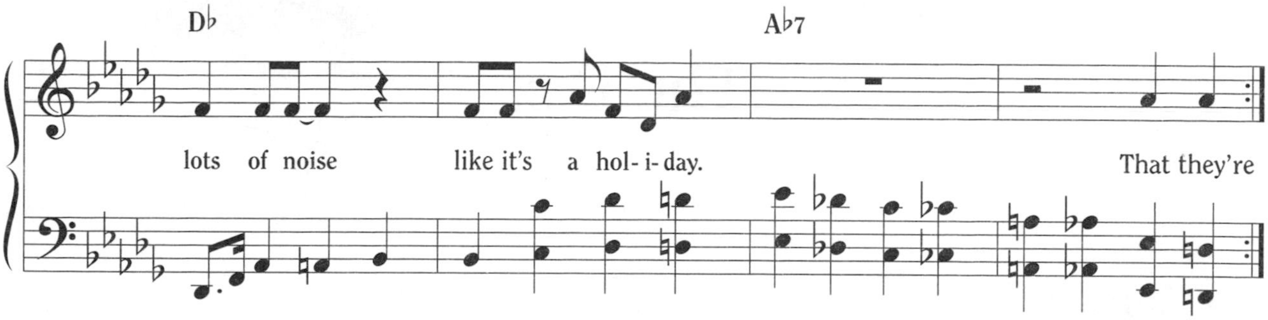
D♭
A♭7
lots of noise like it's a hol- i- day.
That they're

Chorus

2. Some quack, some squeak,
some are quiet when they speak.
There are those who trumpet, "Get out of the way!"
They're big, they're small,
some are short, some are tall,
but whatever they are,
it's safe for us to say that they're…

Chorus

The Fox

Arranged by George James

Lively

The fox went out— on a chill- y night. He prayed for the moon to give him light, for he'd man - y a mile to go that night be - fore he'd reach the town - o, town - o, town- o,— man-y a mile to go that night be - fore he'd reach the town - o.

2. He ran 'til he came to a great big bin
   where the geese and ducks was kept therein.
   "A couple of you will grease my chin
   before I leave this town-o, town-o, town-o.
   A couple of you will grease my chin
   before I leave this town-o."

3. He grabbed the gray goose by the neck,
   he threw the duck across his back,
   he didn't mind the quack, quack, quack,
   and the legs all dangling down-o, down-o,
      down-o…

4. Old Mother Flipper-Flopper jumped out
      of bed.
   Out of the window she stuck her head,
   crying, "John, John, the gray goose is gone
   and the fox is on the town-o, town-o,
      town-o…"

5. John, he ran to the top of the hill,
   blew his horn both loud and shrill.
   The fox said, "I'd better flee with my kill
   or they'll soon be on my trail-o, trail-o,
      trail-o…"

6. He ran 'til he came to his home den.
   There were the little ones, eight, nine, ten.
   They said, "Daddy, better go back again,
   'cause it must have been a mighty fine town-o,
      town-o, town-o…"

7. Now the fox and his wife without any strife
   cut up the goose with a fork and knife.
   They never had such a supper in their life,
   and the little ones chewed on the bones-o,
      bones-o, bones-o…

7

Eensy Weensy Spider

Arranged by George James

I Had a Little Rooster

Arranged by George James

2. I had a little hen by the barnyard gate
   and that little hen was my playmate,
   and that little hen said, "Chick, chick, chick,"
   and that little rooster said, "Cock-a-doodle-doo,
   doo, doo, doo, doo, doo, doo, doo, doo, doo, doo."

3. I had a little duck …   "Quack, quack, quack,"
   and that little hen said …
   and that little rooster said …

4. I had a little pig …   "Oink, oink, oink,"
   and that little duck said …
   and that little hen said …
   and that little rooster said …

11

A Fly Walked In

Arranged by George James

stuck out his tongue at the gro - cery man, and then he walked out of the

store a - gain, a - lone, all a - lone.

2. A fly walked into the barber shop,
   alone, all alone.
   For a haircut he did stop,
   alone, all alone.
   He walked on the comb, put his feet
   on the chair,
   as the barber said, "You don't have any hair."
   The fly, he walked right out of there,
   alone, all alone.

3. A fly walked into the butcher's store,
   alone, all alone.
   He slipped all around on the sawdust floor,
   alone, all alone.
   He sat on the ham, put his feet on the chop.
   The butcher thought he would never stop.
   Then out of there he decided to hop,
   alone, all alone.

Unicorn

Freely

Arranged by George James

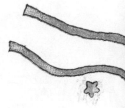

Once up-on an-o—ther day, long a-go and

far a-way, in a wood near a wa—ter spray a

Chorus

un-i-corn came out to play. Un-i-corn,

un—i-corn, pret-ti-est beast that ev-er was born,

spark-ling white from tail— to horn, what's be-come of the

un — i - corn?

2. In another part of the lonely wood
   a cyclops prowled up to no good.
   His one eye peered from the middle of
      his head.
   He was hungry and it was time to be fed.

3. He saw the unicorn standing there
   and silently crept out from his lair,
   when suddenly to his great surprise
   the unicorn looked up with fearful eyes.

Chorus

4. The cyclops froze right where he stood
   and love found its way into that dark wood.
   The unicorn flashed a mysterious smile
   and a tear fell from the cyclops' only eye.

5. "Ah-ha, my friend," the unicorn said,
   "why is that eye in the middle of your head?
   Rather than see you so forlorn
   I'd gladly give up my only horn."

6. Then a flash of light never seen since
   and the cyclops turned into a two-eyed
      prince.
   The unicorn without his horn, of course,
   became the prince's favorite horse.

Chorus

Kookaburra

Reggae

Coda only: repeat and fade

Arranged by George James

Koo- ka, koo- ka- bur - ra, Koo- ka- bur- ra sits in the old gum tree,___ mer- ry mer- ry king of the bush is he.___ Laugh, koo- ka- bur- ra, laugh, koo- ka- bur- ra, gay your life must be.

2. Kookaburra, he's such a royal bird.
   Kookaburra, it's such a funny word.
   Laugh, kookaburra, laugh, kookaburra,
   happy as can be.

3. Kookaburra sits in the old gum tree
   eating all the gumdrops he can see.
   Stop, kookaburra, stop, kookaburra,
   leave some there for me.

Repeat last line.

Repeat last line of verse 1, twice.

16

A Froggy Went A-Courtin'

Arranged by George James

2. He rode up to Miss Mousie's door, uh, huh!
   He rode up to Miss Mousie's door, uh, huh!
   He rode up to Miss Mousie's door,
   and he knocked so hard that his fist got sore, uh, huh! Uh, huh!

3. He took Miss Mousie on his knee, uh, huh!…
   and he said, "Miss Mousie, will you marry me, uh, huh! Uh, huh!"

4. Miss Mousie said, "I'm filled with pride, uh, huh!"…
   and I will be your happy bride, uh, huh! Uh, huh!"

5. Oh, where will the wedding supper be, uh, huh?…
   Way down yonder in a hollow tree, uh, huh! Uh, huh!

6. Now, the first to come was a little white moth, uh, huh!…
   Around her neck was a tablecloth, uh, huh! Uh, huh!

7. The next to come was an old red hen, uh, huh!…
   She played a little tune and she played it again, uh, huh! Uh, huh!

8. Next to come was a nice brown cow, uh, huh!…
   She tried to dance but she didn't know how, uh, huh! Uh, huh!

9. They all gathered 'round the lucky pair, uh, huh!…
   Singing and dancing everywhere, uh, huh! Uh, huh!

I Had a Little Dog

Arranged by George James

Walking song

had a lit-tle dog and his name was Paul. _____ *(Whistle or hum)*

gave him a lit-tle but he want-ed it all. _____ *(Whistle or hum)*

fine

2. I had a little dog
and his name was Maynard.
I gave him an inch,
but he took a whole yard.

3. I had a little dog
and his name was Cheers,
and his legs ran to paws,
and his head ran to ears.

4. I had a little dog
and his name was Rover,
and when he was shedding,
he shedded all over.

5. I had a little dog
and her name was Billie,
and when she dressed up,
she sure acted silly.

6. I had a little dog
and her name was Honey.
When she gave you her paw,
she looked at you funny.

I Wish

Arranged by George James

2. I wish I were a squirrel so fat,
   a real good squirrel I'd be,
   and just before the sun went down,
   I'd climb up the old oak,…
   climb up the old oak tree.

3. I wish I were a pig in the dirt,
   a real good pig I'd be,
   and just before the sun went down,
   I'd sit by the old oak,…sit by the old oak tree.

4. And if I were a mole in the ground,
   a real good mole I'd be.
   You'd find me when the sun went down,
   under the old oak,…under the
   old oak tree.

Animal March

Arranged by George James

March

Woodblock:

Spoken

Al - li - ga - tor, hedge - hog, ant - eat - er, bear, rat - tle - snake, buf - fa - lo, an - a - con - da, hare.

2. Bullfrog, woodchuck, wolverine, goose,
   whippoorwill, chipmunk, jackal, moose.

3. Mud turtle, whale, glowworm, bat,
   salamander, snail, and a Maltese cat.

4. Black squirrel, fox, opossum, wren,
   red squirrel, loon, and a prairie hen.

5. Polecat, dog, wild otter, rat,
   pelican, hog, dodo, and bat.

6. Eagle, kangaroo, sheep, duck, and widgeon,
   conger, armadillo, beaver, seal, pigeon.

7. Reindeer, black snake, ibex, nightingale,
   martin, wild drake, crocodile, and quail.

8. House rat, toe rat, white bear, doe,
   chickadee, peacock, bobolink, and crow.

Boa Constrictor

Chorus

2. Make haste, he's got my waist.
   Be calm, he's got my arm.
   That's grand, he's got my hand.
   That bum, he's got my thumb.

Chorus

3. Oh, yes, he's got my chest.
   Oh, heck, he's got my neck.
   Hey, Ted, he's got my head.
   I said, Ted, he's got my head!

Five Little Monkeys

Arranged by George James

Fast

Five lit-tle mon — keys jump-in' on the bed, one fell off and

bumped his head. Ma-ma called the doc - tor and the doc-tor said,

"No more mon-key bus' - ness jump-in' on the bed."

2. Four little monkeys jumpin' on the bed,
   one fell off and bumped his head.
   Mama called the doctor and the doctor said,
   "No more monkey bus'ness jumpin' on the bed."

3. Three little monkeys …

4. Two little monkeys …

5. One little monkey …

6. No more monkeys jumpin' on the bed,
   no more monkeys bumpin' their head.
   No more calling doctors, and doctors no more said,
   "No more monkey bus'ness jumpin' on the bed."

28

Tailor and the Mouse

Reggae ballad

Arranged by George James

There was a tai-lor who had a mouse, hi - did-dle un - kum fee - dle. They lived to - geth - er in one house, hi - did-dle un - kum fee - dle.

sim.

Chorus

Hi - did-dle un - kum, ta - rum, tan - tum, through the town of

Ram - sey, hi - did-dle un - kum o - ver the sea,

hi - did-dle un - kum fid-dle dee dee.

fine

2. The tailor had a tall silk hat,
   Hi-diddle unkum feedle.
   The mouse he ate it, fancy that!
   Hi-diddle unkum feedle.

Chorus

3. The tailor thought the mouse was ill,…
   He gave him part of a big blue pill,…

Chorus

4. The tailor thought the mouse would die,…
   So he baked him up an apple pie,…

Chorus

5. The mouse he ate it and got all better,…
   He sent the tailor a thank-you letter,…

Chorus

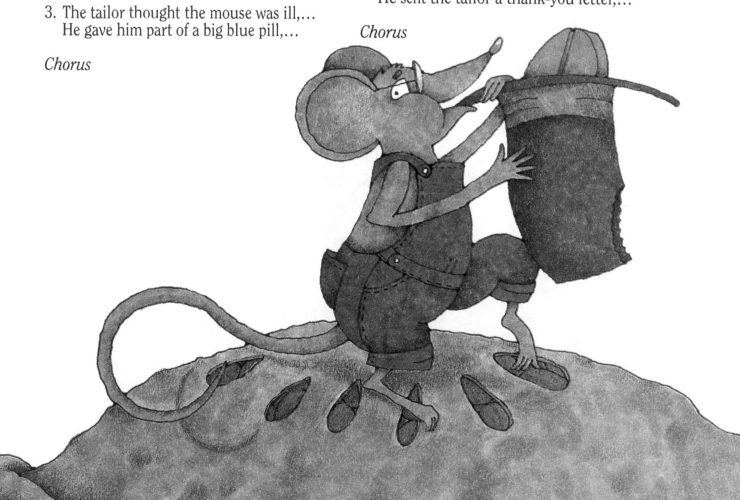

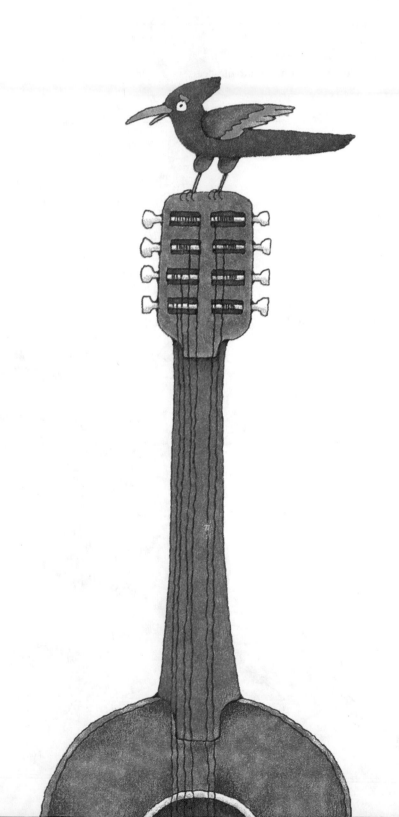